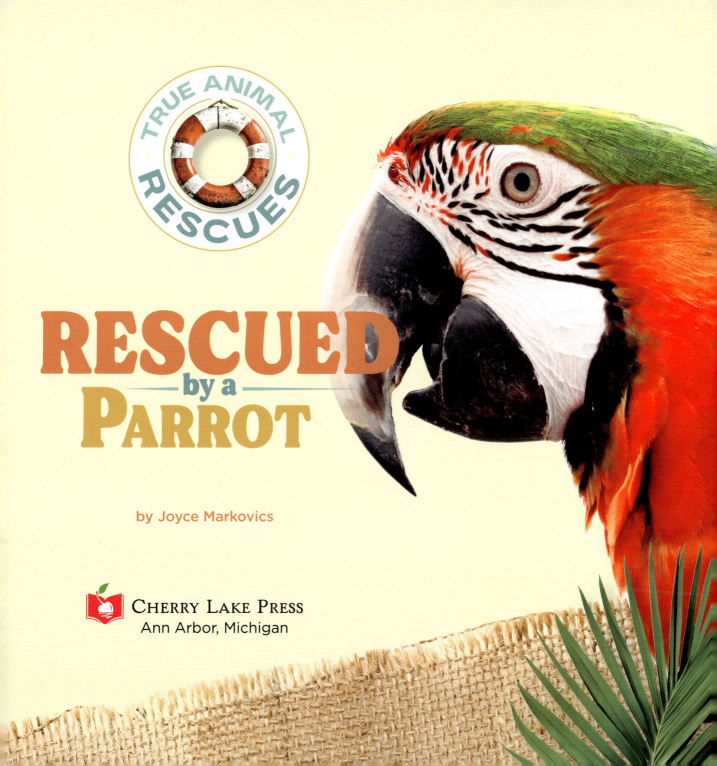

TRUE ANIMAL RESCUES

RESCUED by a PARROT

by Joyce Markovics

CHERRY LAKE PRESS
Ann Arbor, Michigan

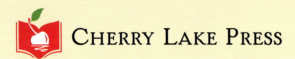

Published in the United States of America by Cherry Lake Publishing
Ann Arbor, Michigan
www.cherrylakepublishing.com

Reading Adviser: Beth Walker Gambro, MS Ed., Reading Consultant, Yorkville, IL

Book Designer: Ed Morgan
Book Developer: Bowerbird Books

Photo Credits: © Nataliya Derkach/Shutterstock, cover; freepik.com, title page and table of contents; © Prostock-studio/Shutterstock, 4–5; © oodles/Shutterstock, 5 bottom; freepik.com, 6; © rima das mukherjee/Shutterstock, 7 top; freepik.com, 7 bottom; © lunopark/Shutterstock, 8; freepik.com, 9; © VH-studio/Shutterstock, 11; © Tatyana Soares/Shutterstock, 12–13; © Audio und werbung/Shutterstock, 14–15; © Sanit Fuangnakhon/Shutterstock, 15 bottom;freepik.com, 16–17; © Flystock/Shutterstock, 19; © Sanit Fuangnakhon/Shutterstock, 20–21.

Copyright © 2026 by Cherry Lake Publishing Group

All rights reserved. No part of this book may be reproduced or utilized in any form or by any means without written permission from the publisher.

Cherry Lake Press is an imprint of Cherry Lake Publishing Group.

Library of Congress Cataloging-in-Publication Data has been filed and is available at catalog.loc.gov.

Printed in the United States of America

Note from publisher: Websites change regularly, and their future contents are outside of our control. Supervise children when conducting any recommended online searches for extended learning opportunities.

Contents

Pearly the Hero 4
Willie and Hannah 10
Charlie the Guard Bird 14
Wonderful Wunsy 18

Profile: Parrot Rescuers 22
Glossary 23
Find Out More 24
Index 24
About the Author 24

Pearly the Hero

It was nighttime in January 2014. Laurajean Niesel and her partner Dave climbed into bed in their Florida home. They quickly drifted off to sleep. In the middle of the night, they heard a loud noise. It was so loud it woke them from their **slumber**. The racket was coming from their pet Indian ring-necked parrot, Pearly. "I heard the bird squawking and flapping its wings," said Laurajean. Pearly was often loud but never at this hour.

Pearly is an Indian ring-necked parrot like this one. These birds are popular pets. They can learn to copy human speech.

Laurajean and Dave got out of bed to check on Pearly. "You could tell something was wrong," Laurajean said. The couple walked toward the screaming bird. But something else caught their attention. "I saw the smoke coming from the laundry room," Laurajean said. Panicked, she called 911. The couple grabbed their parrot and bolted out of the house. Pearly had alerted them to a fire before the smoke alarm!

Fire detectors can save lives.

A ring-necked parrot can be as loud as a chainsaw.

7

In a flash, fire trucks arrived and put out the blaze. Laurajean and Dave watched from across the street. Thanks to Pearly, the family was unharmed. And their home was not destroyed. "I feel very lucky," said Laurajean. "Pearly saved us."

Fire trucks can spray 1,000 to 2,000 gallons (3,785 to 7,571 liters) of water per minute.

Before the fire, Dave found the parrot's squawking annoying. "I'll be a little more **tolerant** of it now," Dave said. "It was really fortunate to have him there." Pearly the parrot is now the family hero.

Parrots can grow very close to their owners.

Willie and Hannah

Pearly isn't the only hero parrot. Willie is another. He's the beloved pet of Colorado **resident** Megan Howard. One morning in 2009, Megan was babysitting 2-year-old Hannah Kuusk in her home. Hannah was enjoying breakfast. That's when Megan briefly left the toddler to use the bathroom.

Out of nowhere, Willie started flapping his wings and yelling. "Mama, baby!" he said. "Mama, baby!" He repeated himself until Megan came running.

Willie is a Quaker parrot. Quaker parrots are small birds known for their ability to talk. They can learn as many as 50 words!

A Quaker parrot weighs about as much as a small apple.

When Megan reached Hannah, the child was blue. She was choking on her breakfast. Megan grabbed the girl. Then she performed **abdominal thrusts**. Megan cleared Hannah's **airway**, saving the toddler.

Quaker parrots are very social. They need to interact with people daily.

After the **incident**, Hannah's family praised Megan. But she believes Willie deserves all the thanks. He's the one who called for help. Hannah's mother still gets upset thinking about what happened. "My heart drops in my stomach," she said. But more than that, her heart is full of thanks for Willie and Megan.

Willie the parrot got a lifesaver award from the **Red Cross**. He was also honored by Colorado's governor!

13

Charlie the Guard Bird

Another parrot lifesaver is Charlie. Early one morning in Arkansas, Jack Dukes heard knocking at his door. Thinking it was a neighbor, he opened it. Only then did he realize his terrible mistake. Two men burst into his home. One hit Jack. The force "knocked me back across the table," Jack remembers. Then the **intruders** looked for things to steal. That's when Jack's scarlet macaw Charlie flew into action.

Scarlet macaws are one of the largest parrots. Their wingspan is more than 3 feet (0.9 meters)!

Charlie attacked the intruders. He screamed, squawked, and clawed at them. And then Charlie bit the men with his powerful beak. Jack said he tore "a chunk of skin" from one of the thieves. After that, Jack heard them say, "Let's get out of here." And the men fled.

Jack couldn't be more grateful to his buddy, Charlie. He credits the parrot with saving his life. To show his thanks, Jack showers Charlie with love. And he spoils the macaw with his favorite food—banana pudding.

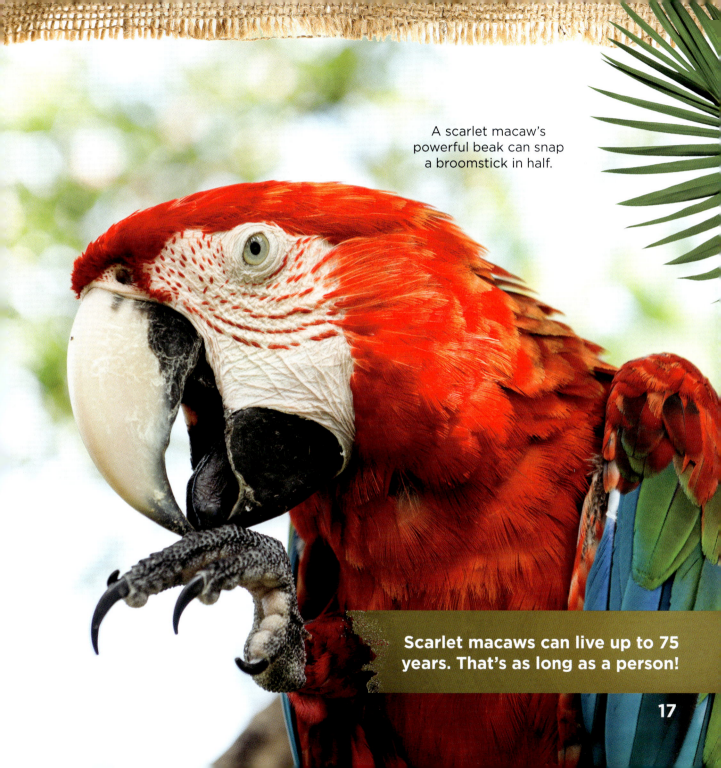

A scarlet macaw's powerful beak can snap a broomstick in half.

Scarlet macaws can live up to 75 years. That's as long as a person!

Wonderful Wunsy

Like Charlie, Wunsy the parrot fights crime. One sunny day in 2014, Wunsy's owner, Rachel Mancino, went for a walk in the park. Wunsy was perched on her shoulder. As she strolled, a man came from behind. "He just jumped on me and was pushing me down," Rachel said. "My heart was thumping. It was so scary," she said.

In a split second, Wunsy reacted. She flew up, flapping her wings in the attacker's face. At the same time, she screeched loudly. The startled attacker ran off.

Wunsy is a type of parrot called an African grey. These parrots are highly intelligent.

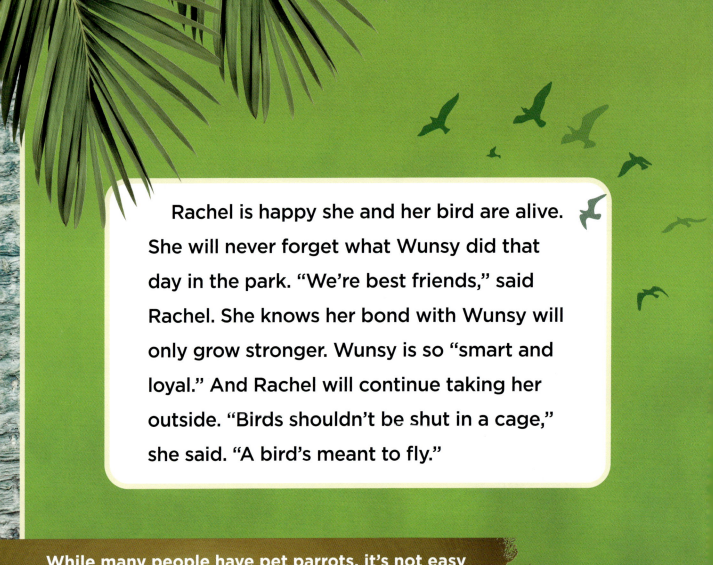

Rachel is happy she and her bird are alive. She will never forget what Wunsy did that day in the park. "We're best friends," said Rachel. She knows her bond with Wunsy will only grow stronger. Wunsy is so "smart and loyal." And Rachel will continue taking her outside. "Birds shouldn't be shut in a cage," she said. "A bird's meant to fly."

While many people have pet parrots, it's not easy caring for them. They require a lot of attention and affection to stay happy and healthy.

Parrots, including African greys, have powerful wings and can fly long distances.

PROFILE:
Parrot Rescuers

Why do some parrots rescue and protect people? Here are some amazing parrot qualities that could explain why.

Social

Parrots are highly social. They bond with other birds and humans. Without friends, parrots can become stressed. Very stressed birds often pluck out their own feathers.

Intelligent

The smartest parrot, an African grey named Alex, is said to have had the intelligence of a 6-year-old. Some parrots know as many as 1,000 words! They can also make and use tools.

Creative

Parrots can learn and imitate sounds to adapt to their environments. They can also solve difficult problems in various ways—like humans!

Glossary

abdominal thrusts (ab-DOM-uh-nuhl THRUHSTS)
an emergency action performed on a person who is choking by pressing down on the person's upper stomach in order to force out food from his or her windpipe

airway (AIR-way)
the passage by which air reaches a person's lungs and allows them to breathe

incident (IN-sih-duhnt)
an event or occurrence

intruders (in-TROOD-urhz)
people who enter a place without permission

Red Cross (RED KRAWS)
an international organization that helps people during wars or natural disasters such as hurricanes or earthquakes

resident (REZ-uh-duhnt)
a person who lives in a certain place

slumber (SLUM-buhr)
to sleep

tolerant (TOL-ur-uhnt)
to put up with something annoying or unpleasant

Find Out More

BOOKS

Markovics, Joyce. *Amazing Animal Minds: Birds*. Ann Arbor, MI: Cherry Lake Press, 2024.

Markovics, Joyce. *Champs! Inspirational Animals: Brave Birds*. Ann Arbor, MI: Cherry Lake Press, 2024.

Recio, Belinda. *When Animals Rescue*. New York, NY: Skyhorse Publishing, 2021.

WEBSITES

Explore these online sources with an adult:

Britannica Kids: Parrot Family

National Geographic: Parrots

Smithsonian Magazine: 14 Fun Facts About Parrots

Index

African grey parrot, 19, 21
Arkansas, 14
beak, parrot, 16–17
Charlie the parrot, 14–18
choking, 12
Colorado, 10, 13
Dukes, Jack, 14, 16
fire, 6, 8
fire trucks, 8
Florida, 4
Howard, Megan, 10, 12–13
Indian ring-necked parrot, 4–5

intruders, 14, 16
Kuusk, Hannah, 10, 12–13
Mancino, Rachel, 18, 20
Niesel, Laurajean and Dave, 4, 6, 8–9
Pearly the parrot, 4–10
Quaker parrot, 10–11
Red Cross, 13
scarlet macaw, 14–15, 17
talking, parrot, 10–11
toddler, 10, 12
Willie the parrot, 10, 12–13
Wunsy the parrot, 18–20

About the Author

Joyce Markovics is drawn to stories that tug at her heart. When she's not writing books for kids, she volunteers at an animal sanctuary where dozens of different species peacefully coexist.